THE 10 LAWS OF POWER

A Lawyer's Manifesto

P O W E R

By **Martin V. Asatrian, Esq.**

Speakeasy Publishing
73-03 Bell Blvd, #10
Oakland Gardens, NY 11364
www.speakeasypublishinginc.com

Ordering Information:

Quantity sales. Special discounts are available on quantity purchases by corporations, associations, and others. For details, contact the publisher at the address above.

Orders by U.S. trade bookstores and wholesalers. Please contact Speakeasy Publishing: Tel: (888) 991-2766 or visit www.speakeasypublishinginc.com.

Printed in the United States of America.

Published in 2019.

ISBN: 978-1-951149-16-1

FOREWORD

I wrote this book to express my concern with the modern legal system. The Courts have more than ever favored the wealthy and well-connected litigants. The working class does not have a chance in a legal system that has abandoned equity, justice, and fundamental fairness for judicial expediency. The large multi-national corporations defended by the law firms with over 1,000 lawyers have steamed rolled litigants with meritorious cases. Criminal defendants have to plea guilty to offenses they did not commit for lack of money, resources and proper representation. The inequity in the legal system has created a population of litigants that cannot get justice. Immigrants are being removed or deported and separated from their families. Fathers cannot obtain proper visitation of their children or custody and mothers have to deal with child support staffers that do not properly enforce.

The only solution is for lawyers to fight the good fight. Utilize the 10 Laws of Power and correct some of the wrongs in the courtroom.

DEDICATION

I dedicate this book to all those lawyers who fight for their clients in the trenches. I hope it is a wake-up call to solo practitioners and small practice lawyers to fight back harder, do not get intimidated by the big law firms.

In particular, I dedicate this book to the countless lawyers that work 60 to 80-hour work weeks and fight for their clients. They are nameless and fearless for a reason. This is not a dedication to the empty suits that always remind us that they are a partner at some large law firm, that they sponsor golf outings, and they vacation in St. Bart's. These are the sell outs that need to be soundly defeated in the courtroom. The 10 Laws of Power if utilized properly will wipe the smirks off the faces of these so called "corporate" lawyers. In the end, they are nothing but highly paid slaves in expensive suits. Knock them out!

DISCLAIMER

This publication is intended to be used for educational purposes only. No legal advice is being given, and no attorney-client relationship is intended to be created by reading this material. The author assumes no liability for any errors or omissions or for how this book or its contents are used or interpreted or for any consequences resulting directly or indirectly from the use of this book. For legal or any other advice, please consult an experienced attorney or the appropriate expert.

Asatrian Law Group, LLC
15 Warren Street
Hackensack, NJ 07601
(201) 663-3164
www.asatrianlaw.com

TABLE OF CONTENTS

About The Author

My name is Martin V. Asatrian and I am the managing and founding member of the Asatrian Law Group. This book is essentially a sequel to my book Only In America, which is about some of the adversaries I and many others faced while emigrating from the Soviet Union. I came to the US with the status of a refugee and was fortunate enough to attend law school at New York University. At a very young age, I dreamt of becoming an attorney, and for the past 20 years I've been able to live out that dream. I am currently of counsel to a larger firm and specialize in areas such as complex civil litigation.

Who Is This Book For?

This book is for every single individual who comes out of law school with an idealistic outlook on thriving and surviving in the modern workplace. It is also for experienced lawyers, because regardless of how many years a lawyer has been practicing, they're still vulnerable to the power games that exist. Within this book, I discuss 10 laws and one bonus law, as well as all modes of power that were exercised against me when I was vulnerable and naïve. Unlike the first book, this one dives into the human condition and how people can be vulnerable to manipulation and deceit from people who pose as friends. This is a realistic, practical book containing laws that can be applied to everyday problems; following these laws can turn a mediocre attorney into an excellent attorney.

Is This Book Just For Other Attorneys Or For Other Professionals As Well?

This book is for the hedge fund professional who's working on Wall Street and not getting ahead, and it will likely open their eyes to why they aren't getting ahead. Some of these laws will help them understand what's really going on behind closed doors. I am not a conspiracy theorist; I am a realist, and I have been around the block. This book is also for doctors, accountants, and every individual who goes to work every day and tries to get ahead but is frustrated because they feel as though doing so is impossible—not because of their lack of skill or hard work, but because of their lack of knowledge and the subtle power games that go on.

What Was Your Vision Behind Some Of These Chapter Titles?

The goal was to make the chapter titles simple and catchy, but the hope is that the actual content within each chapter will lead to many epiphanies that will end up bettering people's lives. Reading this book is not going to solve anyone's problems, but it will definitely increase people's awareness and motivate them to be more serious about their life so that they do not get treated like pawns, but like masters.

CHAPTER 1

BE READY TO DIE

What Do You Mean By Be Ready To Die?

I have found that whether it's a legal adversary or a colleague, the easiest way to let an adversary know that you're not playing games and that you really want to achieve a great result for your client is to show them that the stakes are higher for you than they are for them, that you are prepared to make more sacrifices than they are, that you love and respect your client more than they do, that you have bigger fish to fry, and that you have an ability to rise above simple and monotonous legal practices. Showing these characteristics to your competitors will give you an advantage over them because they will understand that you're not part of the game and you're not like others; you have convictions, you have integrity, and you don't necessarily have to be nice about anything—you just have to be clear about the fact that you are prepared to win. In fact, you hate losing. 'Be ready to die' is a competitive mantra for telling people that you need to win and hate to lose.

Do You Have Some Examples Of How You As An Attorney Have Been All In And Willing To Sacrifice More Than Your Adversary, And How That Played Out For You?

During my third or fourth year of practicing law, I had to deal with a lot of arrogant insurance and malpractice defense lawyers who didn't know who I was because I didn't have a reputation or a name. As a result, they thought that it would be okay to be condescending toward me. This is what showed me that they were weak, because no one should be condescending to anyone, especially to people they don't know. The flip side to that is to show them that they can be as condescending as they want, but you are dead serious, you're going to win, and you think they're soft. I don’t mean soft as in literally soft, but as in concerned about keeping the status quo and the lifestyle they’ve developed. Many of these lawyers forget how they got to where they are; they were probably hard early on but over the years began to rest on their laurels, stop following up on their legal education, and eventually became soft. The younger breed then comes up and hands their heads to them. In one case I handled, my adversary overestimated themselves and underestimated me, and as a result, they lost a substantial profit. There are many other examples in law and business where people tend to underestimate their adversaries at their own peril.

One thing you can draw from the ‘be ready to die’ law is that it can sometimes be wise to let your adversaries believe you’re not as sharp as you truly are, as this could have the effect of luring them in and playing possum, which could lead them to get sloppy. Once that has happened, you can overwhelm them with your skill, legal knowledge, and confidence. This is what will give you a competitive advantage and a greater chance of winning. For example, let’s assume you are in a bar and someone says a bad thing to you; they don't realize that you're a black belt in Jujitsu and they keep bullying you and you allow them to bully you. But then you realize that you're so confident that you could actually put them in a chokehold and put them to sleep. When someone suddenly realizes that they messed with the wrong person, it can be a terrorizing feeling. This is one power game that goes on back and forth, and most people get intimidated, back off, and defer. The ‘be ready to die’ law reminds you to never back off or defer to any lawyer, adversary, or colleague, because no one is better than you. Death before dishonor!

CHAPTER 2

IT'S WAR, NOT A GAME!

What Does It Mean To Say That It's War, And Not A Game?

There is so much at stake in this area of the law. It's not a game where people win and lose and there are no consequences; we must go in with the attitude that losing is not an option, and that's where the war mentality comes from. I always recommend collaborating with your adversaries, but when they are inflexible and uncompromising, you need to take the warrior mentality. Once you take the warrior mentality, there's no looking back; you really have to go in and win. Ultimately, it is your client who benefits from the warrior mentality.

What Are Some Real Examples Of How Attorneys Should Use War Strategies In The Courtroom On Behalf Of Their Clients?

Most capable attorneys that I have dealt with from large firms are very good litigators, but they confuse two terms. They are tacticians, which means that they apply and deploy certain skillsets at trial and during oral arguments. Generals, on the other hand, are the strategists and visionaries who think long-term. You need to be a good tactician and a good strategist. Good generals are strategists too, and in the history of all generals, there are many common threads, one of which is the ability to conquer the enemy within. These people are usually on your side of the camp and are actual turncoats. The enemy within is your own mindset in which you tell yourself you cannot win the war. You need to eradicate your negative mindset or the enemy within, because if you have a positive, warrior-like attitude, then you will be more likely to survive in the context of actual conventional warfare. It's also sometimes important to be nonconventional and unpredictable in the strategies you deploy.

Should An Attorney Or Professional Take Their Business Personally, Or Would That Be A Source Of Liability In The War, So To Speak?

You should never take your cases too personally, but you need to do your best in fighting for your client. You have to be a zealous advocate in your case but you have to leave that in the courtroom when you walk out. With that said, if during a trial or during the course of litigation your integrity as a lawyer is being attacked, then you have to take it personally. This is because in law, all you have is a name and a reputation, and if your adversary or anyone else tries to take that away from you, you must fight harder than you ever have in order to protect it. Once your reputation as a lawyer is besmirched, you're done.

CHAPTER 3

BE UNPREDICTABLE

What Do You Mean By That?

Most people think that they don't have a dark side, but if you study the history of the 20th century, you will come to know that all humans have a dark side. There are 30 million people that are dead as a result of humanity's dark side. If you're aware of it, you can utilize it in a positive way. Having a dark side simply means that you're human, you have flaws, and you have certain traits. The more successful you become in your profession, the more envy and jealousy you will garner from your friends, family, colleagues, and adversaries. People who think they don't have a dark side and play the moral superiority game are the greatest players of all time. They're treacherous because they use moral superiority when their end game is power, and their ultimate end game is tyranny over you.

As An Attorney Or Professional, What Do You Find Is The Harm In Being Predictable? Isn't Predictability A Good Thing?

In any profession, you have to be consistent, but not necessarily predictable. From my standpoint, predictability means that your patterns and routines are so predictable that adversaries know exactly and precisely which direction you're going to go. For example, many hunters choose to only hunt deer because they are predictable and therefore easy to target. Deer have routines and habits, so from a predator's standpoint, they are easier to kill. Only humans have the capacity to be aware of their routines enough to change them. I want to be clear that to be unpredictable does not mean to be erratic. It means to deploy weapons at your disposal in order to win or accomplish a big business deal for your client. Other people will do research on you as an attorney or as a professional before you enter the boardroom, but if you come up with unpredictable ways of thinking outside the box and are actively imaginative, then you will have a competitive advantage. A professional should have multiple personas and never let the other side know which persona is going to be present.

What Do You Mean When You Say You Need To Elevate, Transition, And Pivot As An Attorney Or Any Professional?

Generally speaking, most attorneys do not pivot, transition, or elevate; they're complacent with the lot they have as an attorney, and that's very dangerous. Attorneys need to recreate, relearn, and be willing to enter unfamiliar areas. For example, if you choose to only handle automobile accident cases for 35 years, then you're not really going to grow as a professional. You need to venture into product liability, mass torts, or civil class actions in order to find a new stimulus. Your brain requires that you have a new stimulus in order to grow. I try to recreate myself all the time; sometimes I'm successful, sometimes I'm not. If you're actively trying to recreate yourself and pivot, then you're thinking outside of what 90 percent of people are doing, which is accepting mediocracy. If that's what you want to do in law, then I suggest you leave. You want to be exceptional, extraordinary, and the best of the best.

How Do You Think Being Multidimensional As An Attorney Helps You In Your Professional Career And Personal Life?

When I was a child, both of my parents worked and I basically had a latch key around my neck. As a result, I spent a lot of time exploring parks, playgrounds, and learning about people. I learned that some people are bullies and others cowards, and I always carefully observed them. I was inquisitive and curious, wondering what scared the coward and what the bully was trying to hide. Many of the things I learned as a child play out in the courtroom, and many of my clients can relate to my non-legal experience, which allows us to bond. However, it's important never to be phony; if I can't relate to a client, I won't pretend that I can because they will realize this and won't hire me. It's important to always bring your personal knowledge and insights into the conference room. Ultimately, clients want results, so bring whatever you can to make sure you get those results.

CHAPTER 4

BE OBSESSED!

Why Are Those Who Are Obsessed With What They Do Make Better Lawyers?

Trial lawyers should be obsessed. Friedrich Nietzsche once said, "You can't gain anything unless you pay a social cost or sacrifice." When you're obsessed with a case, you spend a lot of time on it and don't allow yourself to become distracted. Steve Jobs tried to lock himself in a room in order to avoid distractions. For all his personal flaws, the one thing he could was hyper-focus on something, and I think he was obsessed. I'm not saying he was a good person, but his obsession allowed him to excel in his profession. A lawyer who is obsessed with their work is going to do more legal research on their own, know the minutia of the case at hand, and ultimately prevail as a result. You may not be the smartest lawyer in the room, but if you're the most obsessed person in the room, then you're going to have a competitive advantage. Clients want outcomes, and if they see that their lawyer is obsessed, they're going to respect them for it.

Could Being Overly Obsessive Ever Prove To Be A Weakness?

Aristotle said to do everything in moderation. As an attorney, being overly obsessed with one case could prove to be a weakness, particularly if it means paying less attention to your other cases. Be cognizant of your time management, and be careful not to overanalyze cases, because you may not be serving the client as much as you think you are. You have to ensure that you are not serving your own ego.

CHAPTER 5

KILL OR BE KILLED

What Do You Mean By 'Kill Or Be Killed'?

In the legal profession and world of business, there are licensed assassins. There are people who are hired by very wealthy clients to eviscerate you and your client and you need to be aware of that. The law of 'kill or be killed' is really a law of how to protect yourself from these hired guns that are financed by multi-millionaires and billionaires who have all of the resources. These people may have five or six associates under them, and it's hard to deal with that. When dealing with these types of people, it's useful to use their own resources against them. I think you also have to try to get them angry so they make self-inflicted injuries or mistakes. You need to get under their skin and you need to work hard. You must understand that if they win, then they've successfully killed you, which would be bad for your reputation and catastrophic for your client. You need to be keen and self-aware enough to collaborate with other lawyers and find out more about these people in order to address them head on. These people have an enormous amount of power and create inequitable situations, so you have to learn how to fight them in a nonconventional sense and stand up to them in a very strong fashion. If they sense weakness or intimidation, then they will try to kill you, and in this sense, the legal profession is not too different than the animal kingdom.

How Do You Combat Those Who Are Trying To Destroy Your Career Or Case Without Becoming One Of Them?

One technique for combating these professionals is to mirror them. You need to show them that you are willing to 'kill' them in the courtroom. You need to show that you are one of them, because if they know that you are not, then they will try to intimidate you and put you in a submission hold. If they're bringing a knife, then you should bring a gun. You need to show them that you're more capable of destroying them and that they have more to lose. You need to be extra dangerous, and that's where the importance of unpredictability comes in. If you are unpredictable, then you will put them on their heels and create an imbalance. In order to be a good fighter, you need to go for the kill and knock these people out early. Otherwise, they're going to drain you with fatigue and overload you with paperwork. You need to cut out their hearts early, as a figure of speech, because if you don't then they'll cut out yours.

CHAPTER 6

CAN'T KNOCK THE HUSTLE

What Does That Song Mean To You?

I've studied the greatest intellectuals in the history of Western civilization starting with Socrates ending with Jacque Derrida and Michel Foucault. I'm talking about another urban poet by the name of Sean Carter who refers to himself as Jay-Z. I think hip-hop has a lot to offer to the business world and entrepreneurs. Can't Knock the Hustle is a song on Jay-Z's first album Reasonable Doubt, which he made for about 18 people who sold crack during the 80s in the Marcy projects in Brooklyn, New York. People made an enormous amount of money off the sale of crack, which I don't condone whatsoever, but the point is that Jay-Z had a message. Hustle is where I want to focus, because for a lawyer, the hustle is transactional—it's about working and getting results. For the crack dealer, the hustle is transactional and entrepreneurial, but it's also a violation of the law and hurts a lot of people.

From the standpoint of this book, the song means that you can never get soft and that you should always love the process, not just the money or results. I think what Jay-Z was talking about is the adrenaline rush that you get from working hard and earning results. I love the fact that there is an adrenaline rush when you practice law and you're really good at it and money's really not the focus. Instead, the focus is on the actual act of working hard and doing well for your clients. And if you provide value for your clients, then you're probably going to be wealthier yourself. I don't think the words 'money' and 'rich' are dirty words, and I say this because I think some lawyers forget that there's a business dimension to law, which is the need to bring in clients, make connections, and get referrals.

Can't Knock the Hustle is an anthem for working hard 24/7, grinding as much as you can, and never resting on your laurels. If you are never satisfied, then you are always humble and will be hungry at any age, in any practice, and in any profession. In addition, you'll be less likely to get knocked off by the next young buck. Hip-hop is a multibillion-dollar industry that has contributed significantly to our social fabric in America and the world. I've traveled to a lot of places in the world where hip-hop is popular and viewing it as negative or positive thing is a matter of perspective. From my perspective, hip-hop can represent being an entrepreneur and working really hard to get what you want. When you come from extremely poor circumstances to escape, you have to do so through hard work and hustle. Hustle does not necessarily mean falling afoul of the law; it just means being the best at your craft.

Why Is It Okay For Professionals To Use Whatever It Is That Drives Them, Whether It Be Money, Power, Or Material Goods?

Social justice warriors throughout the United States and other places in Western Europe have encouraged the belief in universities that money is a dirty thing and has thereby made the quest for power a dirty thing. Being aggressive or combative is a horrible and distasteful thing, and it's really the fault of the universities. There's nothing wrong with wanting to make more money, take care of your family, and create an education fund for your children. However, there are some people who think they're high and mighty but are really just playing a different game—a power game. They shame people for being driven by money and label them as shallow people, but only because they haven't had to need money. When you are at a point where you can't afford diapers for your children, you realize how important money is. Let's be real for a moment, money gets you security, proper healthcare and a roof over your head. You can't "knock" that it's called existence.

CHAPTER 7

SURVIVAL OF THE FITTEST

What Is The Importance Of Maintaining A Healthy Lifestyle When It Comes To Your Professional Life?

Survival of the fittest is the most important concept for active lawyers, trial lawyers, and CEOs, because I am absolutely convinced that if you engage in several highly intense workouts every week, it will literally change your brain chemistry, increase motivation, and allow you to remain focused and driven. Perhaps most important of all, it will give you confidence in what you do. High-intensity basketball, mixed martial arts, Jujitsu, boxing, and kickboxing are all activities that require a lot of physical contact and will be beneficial to your confidence. With that said, you don't want to be overconfident or cocky. You gain confidence through small, short-term achievements, and if you have enough of these achievements, your dopamine levels will spike and your motivation will increase. Choosing to not work out and choosing an unhealthy diet will have the opposite effect on you, and it will negatively impact your performance as a professional. In turn, it will negatively impact your clients. When looked at in this way, you have a moral duty to work out and be physically in shape.

Is It Important That You Look Good Physically For Your Clients, The Judge, Or The Jury?

At the danger of sounding highly superficial, the truth of the matter is that appearance matters. I think you need to have your suit pressed, you need to make sure you have no stains on your shirt, and you need to have the proper color coordination. Your clothes need to be modern but not too modern, and not too hip. You need to wear dark colors, but can never go wrong with a solid red tie. You need to think about these things because judges, your adversaries, and your clients will. They will look at every centimeter of you. You should also invest in making sure that you look vibrant and healthy. As a professional, your clients are investing a lot of money into you and they want to present a representative who looks sharp. If you can show physical sharpness in addition to mental sharpness, you will win over every client.

Will You Tell The Readers About Your Personal Spiritual Journey And How It Has Impacted You As A Professional?

It is my belief that connecting to a higher source of power through the practice of meditation and yoga will make you a better professional and a better person by putting things into perspective for you. I also think it will balance out some of the rigors and challenges inherent in the practice of law by reminding you that there is something out there that is greater than you. You can also practice gratitude by remembering to appreciate the simplest things in life and perceiving each day as a gift. Spirituality in itself should not be seen as the key to being a successful professional, but as a tool for contributing to the social fabric of your community and bettering who you are as a person.

What Do You Do To Stay Balanced And Fit In All Of The Ways That We Talked About?

I go to bed and wake up early every day, and I believe sleep is extremely important for the release of human growth hormone, health, and weight loss. Each morning, I make a mental checklist of what I want to achieve that day and I try to keep myself accountable for everything I do. I never do everything that is on my checklist because it tends to be too ambitious, but I have a metric for my success and I usually put it higher than what I can actually achieve. I move my standards higher every single day.

From an entrepreneurial standpoint, I have several goals, and if I don't meet them, then I won't let myself leave the office. I put a lot of burdens and pressure on myself, because if I don't, then I'm really not going beyond my comfort zone. Just when I think I'm tired, I will realize that I do have a little bit more left in me. And every day that I push a little harder and go beyond my limits, I get that much closer to achieving my goals. Incremental growth is essential.

I also try to keep my life simple. I have learned to say no to a lot of commitments that I'm not ready for—commitments to which I would have in the past said yes. After work, I go straight to the gym. I also play basketball, hit the bag, do some grappling, and make sure that I try to get physically fit. I make sure I have only salad and a steak, maybe some salmon, but nothing beyond that. I've gotten rid of all sweets and carbs. I've lost 13 or 14 pounds and I feel better.

CHAPTER 8

DON'T GET OUTWORKED

Who's Working On A Case Versus Playing The Crowd? What Has Been Your Experience?

Too many people throw around the word 'genius' too often. There are actual geniuses, but they are few and far between and many people who are referred to as geniuses are not actually geniuses. If you work smart and remain focused, you will be amazed by the amount of work you are able to accomplish. I don't necessarily think it's healthy to work 14 to 16 hours a day, and this will likely just lead to burn out. There are a lot of mind games that go on in litigation and business, so you have to show your adversaries that they need to respect you and that you are serious about your profession. Many mediocre lawyers think they've made it in life because they have a suburban home, car, and other material goods, but they will begin to decline. While they're playing, you're working, which does not mean that you're stuck and trapped in a cubicle in your office, but that you're out rainmaking, getting clients, and bettering yourself as a lawyer.

Is It A Bad Thing To Be On The Hustle, So To Speak, 24/7?

It's not necessarily a bad thing to be on the hustle 24/7. You have to put business opportunities at the top of your list, because doing so could be the difference between making $100,000 a year and $800,000 a year. The person who makes $800,000 will drop everything to pursue a viable business opportunity, and while those people may garner a lot of criticism, they should do it anyway for the betterment of themselves and their family. If you see a business opportunity, you should go after it because it may never arise again.

CHAPTER 9

NOTHING TO LOSE

Is It Good To Have A Lot On The Line With Your Profession, Or Is It Better If You've Nothing To Lose?

It's good to have a lot on the line with your profession, but it's also good to have nothing to lose. At a certain point in your career, you should have a house, car, decent furniture, and other tangibles that are a little above and beyond because you've earned it. At the same time, you should be prepared to take calculated risks and not error on the side of caution and safety. I think this is a cliché, but if you are safe all the time, it's actually risky. You should take more risks in your late 20s and mid-30s than you should in your mid-40s and mid-50s, but if you're in your 30s, you should take the greatest risks. In the legal profession, you should go very hard with risks earlier on in your career because you will really have nothing to lose. During the middle of your career, you should be a moderate risk-taker. Once you get a little bit more established, it's harder to take risks. You will also learn that certain risks are simply fool's gold, while others are opportunities are real and you are a handshake away from a lifechanging meeting. Be kind to strangers, you never know who they are and what they do. Let's be honest, our lifetimes are very short relative to time and space. Aim high, sky's the limit. What do you have to "lose", your life. Some say life is overrated anyway. It is simply a "blink of the eye" absolutely irrelevant relative to the universe and the concept of infinity.

CHAPTER 10

THE ART OF MASTERY, SEDUCTION, AND WAR

The Art Of Mastery, Seduction, And War: What Does It All Mean?

The art of mastery has to do with the fact that you put 10,000 hours of work into your craft. Very few people are very good at the outset unless they have some type of outlier quality. You develop your mastery through hard work, a good mentor, apprenticeship, willingness to do the most tedious tasks, and by gradually increasing your ability to accomplish more serious tasks. When you've reached a point where everything is easy for you, you will have reached a point of mastery, and then you can teach others how to become masters. During this stage of your career, you will see the playing field for what it is, and you'll see it much more clearly than others. Whether you're a stockbroker, hedge fund manager, or CEO, your goal is to become a master. Masters are humble; they're not necessarily arrogant. They also tend to freely share advice and wisdom when asked to do so. If a good master has agreed to take you under their wing as you work your way toward mastery, then consider yourself fortunate. The most successful people in law have had excellent mentors who helped them to become mentors themselves.

I am very big on the art of mastery and understanding what it's like to work under and learn from a master. During the process, you develop very personal relationships with them, and when they pass away, it hurts a lot because they've given you so much; that's the art of mastery and the art of seduction. To be clear, the art of seduction is not about flirtation or manipulation; seduction is inborn. People who have the art of seduction are charismatic, charming, and able to encourage people to not only see but to join their vision. If you have this quality, you should use it for the betterment of your clients; you should use it to charm your adversaries, judges, and potential new clients.

The art of war is about having a warrior mentality, thinking like a general, and formulating short and long-term strategies that you will execute with the use of a team of lieutenants, captains, and sergeants. If you are able to put such a chain of command into action and if you trust your team to do their job, then you will be a good general and a good strategist who is capable of building an empire. Your empire will start with a few people and grow to 800 or more lawyers. You should have a very clear vision of what you want to do, and like most generals, you must weed out the enemies within. There will be many people who are envious of you; you must unmask them and identify their true intentions.

Do Your Clients Or Business Associates Ever Perceive Your Charisma And Charm As Over The Top Or Fake?

It is extremely important to avoid being fake. Charisma and charm should not be calculated; rather than tell people you're charismatic, others should tell you that you are charismatic. The best thing you can do as a charismatic individual is to lay out a vision and get people to follow it. Before you know it, you will have a growing group of followers, and that's how you build your team. As far as clients are concerned, it is extremely dangerous. There should be no charm effect on your clients; you need to be extremely black and white and inform them of the likelihood of success in an analytical way. If they find you charming, that's okay, but you have to actually deliver. With that said, charisma is very good for obtaining new clients and building relationships, because in the end, people want to do business with people they like. If you have a personality that comes off insincere or you tend to talk down to people, that is the opposite of charisma and you're not going to be liked. In order to succeed, you must be liked and like people; if this doesn't sound like you, then I don't think this is the profession for you.

How Do You Know When To Collaborate With Other Professionals, Specialists, Or Experts, As Opposed To Go It Alone?

With collaboration, there's always an inequitable output of work. In other words, one person will work harder than others, and the others will reap the benefits. However, partners with similar talents should collaborate more. If each partner in a collaboration is highly effective and organized individually, then the collaboration will be beneficial. You do need to be very wary of the fact that if you are bringing in the clients, then you are more valuable than someone who isn't bringing in the clients. With that said, I think that the person who does more work but does not necessarily bring in new clients can be more valuable in some ways. Ultimately, I think it is best to have a blend and to ensure that you are not being taken advantage of. Depending on the circumstances, it may be better to collaborate with someone who is highly specialized in their field, and other times it may be better to go it alone. At all times, you should consult with individuals from whom you can learn.

How Do You Gracefully Accept Defeat And Know When The Best Thing To Do Is Throw In The Towel?

Never throw in the towel; if a judge or jury rules against you, you will at least know that you put everything out there that you could. It is your moral duty to reach out to your adversary and congratulate them on their victory; doing this is classy, and when you inevitably deal with them again in the future, they will respect you. Sometimes you will win and sometimes you will lose, but you always need to be a good sport about it.

CHAPTER 11

BE PARANOID

What Does A Healthy Degree Of Paranoia Mean To You?

Bill Clinton once said that even paranoid people have enemies, and I think that as you become increasingly successful in your field, the number of friends that turn into enemies exponentially multiplies. Humans are self-interested and human nature dictates that most people are not going to be happy for people who thrive. That is hard to say, but it's true. This means that you have to watch yourself, because there's nothing greater than the spectacle of watching someone reach the upper limit of their profession only to get smacked down and go to the commoners.

In order to become paranoid, you need to do a little bit of intelligence gathering and find out what people are doing to conspire and compete against you. You need to figure out what people are doing to undercut you, and you cannot isolate yourself. You also need to also use your adversaries' competitiveness to your benefit so that you become a better competitor yourself. You cannot allow other people's envy and jealousy towards you make you stop striving and asking for more from your profession; you should let it fuel you but be careful not to become boastful. You can limit your paranoia by being helpful toward others, but never forget that your colleagues are not your friends; be careful with what you tell them about your personal life, because they could use it against you.

Can You Give Examples Of When A Healthy Dose Of Paranoia Helped To Protect Your Career?

I once had an interaction with a very aggressive and politically connected adversary who flaunted their political connections in the state of New Jersey. This adversary was trying to hurt my reputation by speaking ill of me to my colleagues. The good news about this is that it indicated that I was relevant, otherwise they wouldn't have been talking about me. By having some allies, I was able to learn that this adversary was scheming against me. It is important to never let your adversaries know that you know that they are scheming against you; instead, flatter them and get as close to them as possible. When the time is right, you can exact revenge against them. I use the word revenge unapologetically, because if another person is trying to hurt you, using revenge unapologetically is really just a form of self-defense and a way of communicating that no one can mess with your reputation as a lawyer.

Healthy paranoia is good because it allows you to determine who is and who is not scheming against you. In essence, these are intelligence gathering techniques that the CIA and FBI use. If you don't have allies, you won't know who is scheming against you. At the same time, your allies may be just trying to instigate a fight. This is why it is important to do a lot of your own research, be confident in the identity of your enemy, and then try to eviscerate them before they have a chance to eviscerate you.

CONCLUSION

What Are The Readers Of This Book Going To Take Away From It?

The aim of this book is not to teach people how to manipulate and take advantage of people in the workplace; it is a self-defense guide to survival in the workplace. I want readers to know that some of these laws may not apply to their lives, while some of them may, and sometimes all of them will. I want this book to raise awareness of the fact that the workplace is not a playground. People who are doing well in their profession need to realize that others will be gunning for them. Discovering that you have a growing number of enemies is actually a testament to how well you are doing. I want people to discover that prior to reading this book, they may not have realized that they were being naïve and letting other people's hidden intentions go unnoticed. You need to be wary of everyone—your superiors, people who are lateral to you, legal assistants, associates, and anyone who has a self-interest which isn't the same as your own. I want this book to help people excel, thrive, survive, be defensive, and remain physically fit to deal with the pressures of this extremely challenging and rewarding profession called law.

ACKNOWLEDGEMENTS

I acknowledge those teachers and professors I had from grade school to college and law school. I also acknowledge my parents. My father who always taught me to be respectful and kinds as well as my mother who taught me the importance of taking risks, working hard for her family and some aspects of survival in this dark world.

I acknowledge the philosophers that I read at NYU, Oxford and the University of London. Nietzche taught me to be comfortable with angst and to laugh at concepts of life and death, as well as the need for solitude. Marx taught me that life is unfair, but you can accept your own history by not surrendering but fighting the modes of inequality. Above all, Jean Paul Sartre taught me that life is "meaningless" and all we have is "nothingness" if that is the case, then all we need to do simply observe the "absurdity" of life and accept the inevitable, our own mortality.

NOTES

The only notes I can make in this book is that the 20th century was a century marked by death.

I have never discussed the Armenian Genocide and have never written about it for various reasons. But here I would like to say a few words from a grandson of survivors of the Armenian Genocide. The ghost of the Genocide haunts all the children and grandchildren of survivors.

I implore each survivor, the sons of the Genocide to fight injustice everywhere especially the Courtroom. As an Armenian lawyer, I see all of my client's injustices as my own. That is why we fight. Sure, we get knocked down, but we always get up. To my Armenian brothers, do not cower, rather stand tall, and if you can't get heaven, Raise Hell!

Made in the USA
Monee, IL
18 May 2026

50340491R00033